CLASSIC INDIAN STORIES • PRATILIPI COMICS INDIA •

THE LIFE OF SWAMI VIVEKANANDA

Published by Westland Books, a division of Nasadiya Technologies Private Limited, in 2024

No. 269/2B, First Floor, 'Irai Arul', Vimalraj Street, Nethaji Nagar, Alapakkam Main Road, Maduravoyal, Chennai 600095

Westland and the Westland logo are the trademarks of Nasadiya Technologies Private Limited, or its affiliates.

ISBN: 9789360454487

10 9 8 7 6 5 4 3 2 1

Comic script: Dr Rajeev Tamhankar
Art and lettering: Abhinav Sajan
Operations lead: Angelin Diana
Quality assurance supervisor: Abhigyan Singh
Art direction: Ashiq Shanavas
Creative producer: Dr Rajeev Tamhankar

Printed at Nutech Print Services, India

SEPTEMBER 1893, CHICAGO
AS HE STOOD BEFORE THE VAST GATHERING, HE TOOK A DEEP BREATH, HIS VOICE CALM YET POWERFUL—ABOUT TO DELIVER A HISTORIC SPEECH THAT WOULD RESONATE THROUGH THE AGES—A POWERFUL MESSAGE OF UNITY, TOLERANCE AND THE TIMELESS WISDOM OF AN ANCIENT LAND.
SISTERS AND BROTHERS OF AMERICA, IT FILLS MY HEART WITH JOY UNSPEAKABLE TO RISE IN RESPONSE TO THE WARM AND CORDIAL WELCOME WHICH YOU HAVE GIVEN US.
I THANK YOU IN THE NAME OF THE MOST ANCIENT ORDER OF MONKS IN THE WORLD ...

I THANK YOU IN THE NAME OF THE MOTHER OF RELIGIONS ...
... AND I THANK YOU IN THE NAME OF MILLIONS AND MILLIONS OF HINDU PEOPLE OF ALL CLASSES AND SECTS.
MY THANKS, ALSO, TO SOME OF THE SPEAKERS ON THIS PLATFORM WHO, REFERRING TO THE DELEGATES FROM THE ORIENT, HAVE TOLD YOU THAT THESE MEN FROM FAR-OFF NATIONS MAY WELL CLAIM THE HONOUR OF BEARING TO DIFFERENT LANDS THE IDEA OF TOLERATION.

I AM PROUD TO BELONG TO A RELIGION WHICH HAS TAUGHT THE WORLD BOTH TOLERANCE ...
... AND UNIVERSAL ACCEPTANCE.
THIS IS THE STORY OF SWAMI VIVEKANANDA, WHO ROSE FROM A YOUNG BOY IN CALCUTTA TO SIT AMONG THE SPIRITUAL GIANTS OF THE WORLD—PERHAPS THE ONLY ONE AMONG THEM WITHOUT A PREPARED SPEECH.

SISTERS AND BROTHERS OF AMERICA ...
BUT WHOSE WORDS SWEPT THE WORLD OFF ITS FEET.
THIS IS THE STORY OF THE MAN WHO FEARLESSLY CARRIED THE WISDOM OF THE EAST TO THE WEST.
SWAMI VIVEKANANDA
THE WELL KNOWN HINDU MONK AND DELEGATE TO THE WORLD'S PARLIMENT OF RELIGIONS, WHO GAVE AN ADDRESS IN THIS CITY A YEAR AGO, WILL DELIVER A LECTURE AT UNITY HALL, FRIDAY EVENING
A GLIMPSE INTO THE LIFE OF A VISIONARY WHO BRIDGED CULTURES AND SPARKED A GLOBAL AWAKENING.

BUT SWAMI VIVEKANADA'S STORY BEGINS 30 YEARS AGO, ON 12 JANUARY 1863, IN CALCUTTA, THE CAPITAL OF BRITISH INDIA.
ON THIS COLD, MOMENTOUS MORNING, A SPIRITUAL LEADER, DESTINED TO TRANSFORM THE WORLD, COMES INTO BEING.
NARENDRANATH DATTA IS BORN TO VISHWANATH DATTA AND BHUVANESHWARI DEVI.
THE BABY HAS A VERY POSITIVE AURA.
INDEED.

HE BELONGS TO A TRADITIONAL FAMILY AND IS ONE OF NINE SIBLINGS.
HIS FATHER, VISHWANATH DATTA, IS AN ATTORNEY AT THE CALCUTTA HIGH COURT AND HIS MOTHER A DEVOUT HOUSEWIFE.
HERE! I HAVE PACKED YOUR TIFFIN.
NARENDRA, DON'T TROUBLE YOUR MOTHER TODAY.
DON'T WORRY! I WILL TRY TO TEACH HIM MEDITATION TO CALM HIM DOWN.

NARENDRA IS MISCHIEVOUS AND RESTLESS AS A CHILD. HIS PARENTS OFTEN HAVE DIFFICULTY CONTROLLING HIM.
SIT DOWN HERE, BETA! YOU MUST MEDITATE IN FRONT OF LORD SHIVA.
MEDITATE?
YES, BETA! CLOSE YOUR EYES AND FOCUS ON GOD. THIS WILL HELP YOU CLEAR YOUR MIND.
OKAY, MA!
THUS, NARENDRANATH BECOMES INTERESTED IN SPIRITUALITY FROM A YOUNG AGE. HE'D MEDITATE BEFORE IMAGES OF DEITIES SUCH AS SHIVA, RAMA, SITA AND HANUMAN.

HE IS ALSO DRAWN TO SOCIAL RESPONSIBILITY FROM AN EARLY AGE.
BHIKSHAAM DEHI!
HERE, GURU-JI!
WHY DID YOU GIVE HIM ALL THE RICE?
MA, ISN'T IT RIGHT TO HELP THOSE IN NEED? HE LOOKED SO HUNGRY.
YES, BETA! YOU DID A GOOD DEED.
MA, I'M GOING TO MEDITATE.

AS NARENDRANATH GREW, HE DEVELOPED A PASSION FOR READING, EXPLORING A VAST ARRAY OF SUBJECTS, INCLUDING PHILOSOPHY, RELIGION, HISTORY, SOCIAL SCIENCE, ART AND LITERATURE. HE ALSO STUDIED THE VEDAS, UPANISHADS, BHAGAVAD GITA, RAMAYANA, MAHABHARATA AND THE PURANAS.
BOOKS ARE VALUABLE BUT HOLISTIC DEVELOPMENT IS ESSENTIAL. A SOUND MIND THRIVES BEST IN A SOUND BODY.
HE REGULARLY PARTICIPATED IN PHYSICAL EXERCISE, SPORTS AND EVEN MUSIC.

AT THE AGE OF SIXTEEN, IN 1879, NARENDRANATH STOOD OUT AS THE ONLY STUDENT TO RECEIVE FIRST-DIVISION MARKS IN THE PRESIDENCY COLLEGE ENTRANCE EXAMINATION.
AND HE JOINED THE GENERAL ASSEMBLY'S INSTITUTION, IN CALCUTTA (NOW KNOWN AS THE SCOTTISH CHURCH COLLEGE).
I WILL GET TO STUDY WESTERN PHILOSOPHY, LOGIC AND EUROPEAN HISTORY HERE.
HIS VERSATILITY IMPRESSED EVERYONE, INCLUDING THE PRINCIPAL OF HIS COLLEGE—WILLIAM HASTIE.
NARENDRANATH IS A GENIUS. I HAVE TRAVELLED FAR AND WIDE, YET NEVER MET A YOUNG MAN OF HIS TALENTS AND POTENTIAL—NOT EVEN AMONG THE PHILOSOPHICAL STUDENTS IN GERMAN UNIVERSITIES. HE IS DESTINED TO LEAVE A MARK ON THE WORLD!

NO CHILD MARRIAGE!
WE WILL NOT LET CHILD MARRIAGE HAPPEN!
THEY ARE WORKING ON A RIGHT CAUSE. I MUST JOIN THE RALLY.
FOLLOWERS, I AM HERE TO TELL YOU THAT WE MUST OPPOSE CHILD MARRIAGE AT ALL COSTS! THIS IS INHUMAN.
ISN'T IT TRUE THAT HE GOT HIS OWN DAUGHTER MARRIED TO A RICH MAN WHEN SHE WAS JUST A CHILD?
IF THAT IS TRUE, THEN THIS IS HYPOCRISY.
SIR, MAY I ASK YOU SOMETHING? IS IT TRUE YOU GOT YOUR OWN DAUGHTER MARRIED WHEN SHE WAS A CHILD?

YES, IT'S TRUE!
OH, THEN WHO IS HE TO PREACH TO US?!
YES IT IS!
SUCH A HYPOCRITE!
WAIT! WHERE ARE YOU GOING? LET ME EXPLAIN.
EVERYONE HERE IS JUST EXPLOITING EACH OTHER. WHO CAN TELL ME WHAT IS RIGHT AND WHAT IS WRONG? WHAT IS THE ULTIMATE TRUTH? WHAT IS GOD?
NARENDRA APPROACHES A PANDIT.
SIR, HAVE YOU EVER FELT GOD?
NO, BETA! BUT YOUR EYES HAVE THE LOOK OF A YOGI. IF YOU TRULY DESIRE IT, I AM CERTAIN YOU WILL BE ABLE TO SEE GOD.

ON HIS WAY HOME ...
NARENDRA! NARENDRA! I WAS LOOKING FOR YOU ALL OVER.
WHAT IS IT, SURENDRA?
WE HAD ARRANGED A SANGEET FUNCTION FOR TODAY, AS SHRI RAMAKRISHNA PARAMAHAMSA HIMSELF WILL BE COMING OVER. HOWEVER, THE GENTLEMAN WE INVITED TO SING IS UNABLE TO MAKE IT. PLEASE CAN YOU SING IN HIS PLACE?
BUT ...
PLEASE NARENDRA, I REALLY NEED YOUR HELP.
OKAY. I WILL COME OVER.

AND SO, NARENDRANATH SINGS, WHILE RAMAKRISHNA PARAMAHAMSA WATCHES INTENTLY.
AFTERWARDS ...
NARENDRA! COME TO DAKSHINESHWAR ONCE. I WILL WAIT FOR YOU.
A CONFUSED NARENDRA HAS NO IDEA THAT THIS ONE SIMPLE MEETING WOULD BE THE FOUNDATION OF HIS MONUMENTAL JOURNEY AHEAD.

AT HIS COLLEGE ...
PROFESSOR, MAY I ASK SOMETHING? WHAT IS THE MEANING OF TRANCE?
NARENDRA, TRANCE IS AN EXPERIENCE THAT RESULTS FROM THE PURITY OF MIND THAT RESULTS AFTER CONCENTRATING ON JUST ONE THOUGHT OR OBJECT. I HAVE SEEN ONLY ONE PERSON ATTAIN THE STATE OF TRANCE.
WHO IS THAT, PROFESSOR?
SHRI RAMAKRISHNA PARAMAHAMSA OF DAKSHINESHWAR.
IT IS AS IF THE UNIVERSE IS SENDING SIGNS. A CURIOUS NARENDRA REACHES DAKSHINESHWAR.
I AM GLAD YOU CAME! I WAS WAITING FOR YOU FOR SO LONG. I WANT TO TEACH YOU EVERYTHING THAT I HAVE LEARNT OVER THE YEARS. I KNOW WHO YOU TRULY ARE, NARENDRA. I KNOW THAT YOU ARE NARAYANA HIMSELF.

WHAT IS HE SAYING? I AM NO GOD.
COME, I WANT TO GIVE YOU SOME KHEER.
RAMAKRISHNA BRINGS A BOWL OF KHEER.
HERE, EAT IT! LET ME FEED YOU WITH MY OWN HANDS.
THAKUR, BUT ...
NO BUTS. JUST EAT.
EVERYBODY IN THE WORLD JUST GOES TO GOD AND CRIES. SOME CRY FOR THEIR WIVES OR CHILDREN, SOME FOR MONEY, BUT I LOVE GOD AS IF SHE IS MY MOTHER. YOU SEE THAT TEMPLE? THAT IS MY MA'S TEMPLE. MA KAALI.

HAVE YOU SEEN GOD?
YES, I HAVE. JUST LIKE I SEE YOU, I HAVE SEEN GOD. I SIT WITH GOD AND TALK JUST LIKE I AM TALKING WITH YOU. IF ONE HAS ACHIEVED INNER PEACE, ONE CAN SEE GOD. HERE, HAVE ANOTHER SPOON OF KHEER!
WHEN NARENDRA RETURNS HOME.
COME, BETA! I HAVE MADE SOME KHEER FOR YOU. YOU WERE GONE FOR SO LONG ON YOUR TRIP TO MEET RAMAKRISHNA. COME, I WANT TO FEED YOU WITH MY OWN HANDS TODAY.
JUST LIKE MY MOTHER, RAMAKRISHNA TOO TREATS ME LIKE HIS SON. I MUST MEET HIM AGAIN.

NARENDRANATH RETURNS TO MEET RAMAKRISHNA.
THAKUR, HOW CAN I SEE GOD?
COME! SIT HERE BESIDE ME.

NARENDRA FALLS TO THE GROUND AND STARTS VISUALISING ...
AH! WHAT HAVE YOU DONE, THAKUR? PLEASE, DON'T! I HAVE PARENTS AT HOME.
WHAT WAS THAT? WAS I TRICKED? OR DID I REALLY SEE ...

HAVE SOME KHEER BEFORE YOU LEAVE.
NOT TODAY! BUT I WILL COME BACK SOON, THAKUR.
NARENDRA RETURNS HOME
WHAT IS IT ABOUT HIM THAT KEEPS ATTRACTING ME TO MEET HIM?
YOU'VE BEEN GROWING RESTLESS EVER SINCE YOU MET RAMAKRISHNA. PERHAPS MARRIAGE WOULD BRING YOU THE STABILITY YOU NEED.
FATHER, I DON'T WANT TO GET MARRIED.
NARENDRA IS YET TO SETTLE DOWN. HE MUST FIND A JOB FIRST. HOW WILL HE TAKE CARE OF A FAMILY? WE OURSELVES ARE STRUGGLING FOR MONEY.

BUT GOD HAD OTHER PLANS. FEW DAYS LATER ...
FATHER, YOU LEFT US! THE WORLD WILL NEVER BE THE SAME. HOW WILL ANY OF US COPE WITH THIS LOSS?
HOW WILL OUR FAMILY SURVIVE NOW? WHERE WILL WE FIND THE MONEY? I WILL HAVE TO DO SOMETHING ABOUT THIS.

NARENDRANATH'S WORRIES WERE REAL. THE FAMILY STRUGGLED TO PUT FOOD ON THE TABLE.
MA, HOW MUCH FOOD DO WE HAVE TODAY?
WE HAVE JUST TWO ROTIS. YOU AND YOUR BROTHER CAN EAT. I'M NOT HUNGRY.
NO, MA, MY FRIEND GOPAL HAS ALREADY INVITED ME TO EAT WITH HIM. YOU BOTH PLEASE EAT.
HOW LONG CAN I KEEP LYING ABOUT GETTING FOOD ELSEWHERE? MA WILL FIGURE IT OUT. I NEED TO FIND A WAY TO GET MONEY.
GO AND ASK MA FOR MONEY.
BUT THAKUR ...
PLEASE GO. I INSIST.

MA ... PLEASE GIVE ME ... TRUE KNOWLEDGE.
DID YOU ASK HER FOR MONEY?
I WANTED TO ... BUT I COULDN'T.
YOU COULDN'T?

YES. I DON'T KNOW WHY.
GO AND ASK AGAIN.
MA, MAY I ... ALWAYS BE DEVOTED TO YOU!
I AM UNABLE TO ASK HER FOR MONEY. PERHAPS IT IS NOT IN MY FATE.
EVERYTHING WILL BE ALRIGHT, NARENDRA. I WILL ASK MA TO SHOW YOU THE WAY.

LATER ...
I HEARD HE HAS TAKEN TO DRINKING AND ALL KINDS OF BAD HABITS AFTER HIS FATHER'S DEMISE.
HE GOSSIP REACHES RAMAKRISHNA ...
THAKUR, I HAVE HEARD THAT NARENDRA HAS BEEN DRINKING ALL DAY AND NIGHT.
NO, THIS ISN'T POSSIBLE! I SPOKE TO MA. SHE SAID IT WOULD NEVER HAPPEN.
AND WHAT ARE YOU AND YOUR FRIENDS DOING? NARENDRA, YOUR FRIEND, IS IN DEEP FINANCIAL TROUBLE.
YOU MUST ALL COLLECT MONEY FOR HIM AND HELP HIM THROUGH THIS DIFFICULT PERIOD.
YES.

LATER ...
WHAT IS ALL THIS, FRIEND?
THAKUR MOTIVATED US TO COLLECT MONEY FOR YOU.
NARENDRA EXITS ANGRILY FROM RAMAKRISHNA'S PLACE.
WHAT ELSE COULD I DO? YOU NEEDED MONEY.
NARENDRA EXITS ANGRILY FROM RAMKRISHNA'S PLACE
THAKUR, I KNOW YOU ARE THE ONLY ONE WHO TRUSTS ME WHEN EVEN MY MOTHER AND BROTHER ARE DOUBTING ME. BUT I CANNOT ACCEPT MONEY LIKE THIS.

NARENDRA GOT UPSET WITH THAKUR. THEIR RELATIONSHIP THUS WENT THROUGH MANY UPS AND DOWNS, NARENDRA'S HEART ACHED WITH CONFLICT. HOWEVER, AS YEARS PASSED AND RAMAKRISHNA'S HEALTH DETERIORATED, NARENDRA FELT THE CALL TO RETURN, REALISING THAT LOVE COULD MEND EVEN THE DEEPEST RIFTS.
THAKUR, I WISH TO ATTAIN SAMADHI FOR FOUR DAYS. I WILL ONLY RETURN TO CONSCIOUSNESS WHEN IT'S TIME TO EAT.
I ALWAYS BELIEVED YOU WOULD GROW INTO A GREAT BANYAN TREE, OFFERING WISDOM AND COMFORT TO THOUSANDS. BUT YOU'VE BECOME SELFISH, FOCUSSED ONLY ON YOUR OWN SALVATION, WITH LITTLE CONCERN FOR SHARING THE MESSAGE WITH OTHERS.
I WANTED YOU TO SPREAD THE MESSAGE. BUT YOU ...
LIE DOWN, THAKUR. NARENDRA, PLEASE WAIT OUTSIDE.
NARENDRA, YOU KNOW HE IS SUFFERING FROM THROAT CANCER. HE NEEDS TO REST. HE MUST NOT TALK.

MONTHS LATER ...
NARENDRA, WHY DO YOU LOOK SO SAD? THIS IS MA'S WISH. COME SIT NEAR ME, I WILL SHARE WITH YOU ALL THAT I KNOW.
THESE ARE MY FINAL MOMENTS. LET ME PASS ALL THAT I KNOW TO YOU.

WE ARE JUST A DOZEN DISCIPLES. WE ARE ALL POOR AND NO ONE KNOWS US. HOW WILL WE SPREAD HIS MESSAGE?
WE MUST CARRY FORWARD THAKUR'S MESSAGE TO TREAT EVERYONE AS AN EQUAL AND WITH RESPECT, IRRESPECTIVE OF THEIR CASTE OR CREED. WE WILL TEACH THE COMPASSION OF HINDUS, THE DEDICATION OF SIKHS AND THE BROTHERHOOD OF MUSLIMS TO ALL.
BUT WHO WAS GOING TO LISTEN TO A HANDFUL OF YOUNG MEN? THEY WERE MET WITH CONTINUOUS REJECTIONS.

THE YOUNG MEN MOVE INTO AN ABANDONED HOUSE AND BEGIN LIVING OFF ALMS.

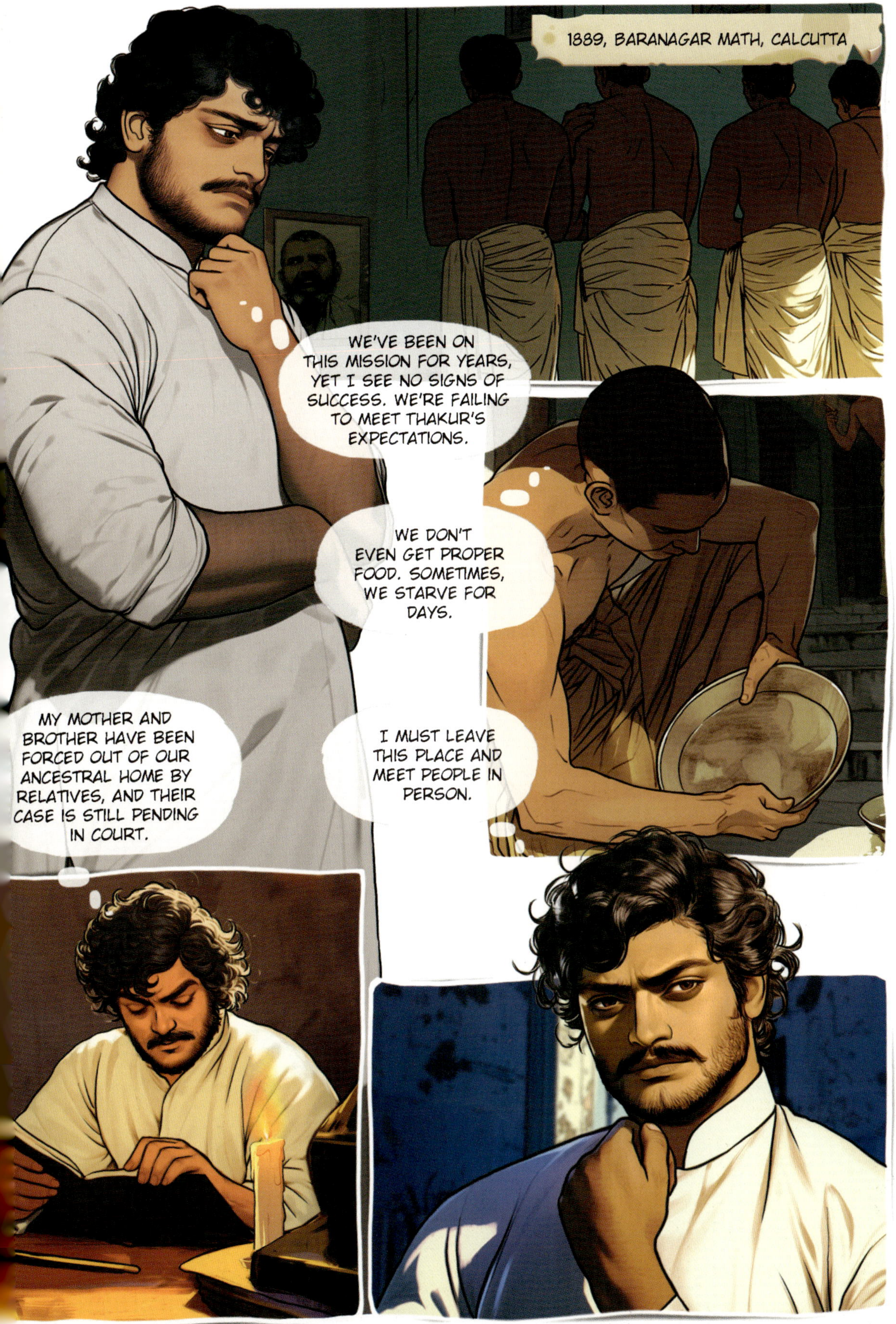
1889, BARANAGAR MATH, CALCUTTA
WE'VE BEEN ON THIS MISSION FOR YEARS, YET I SEE NO SIGNS OF SUCCESS. WE'RE FAILING TO MEET THAKUR'S EXPECTATIONS.
WE DON'T EVEN GET PROPER FOOD. SOMETIMES, WE STARVE FOR DAYS.
MY MOTHER AND BROTHER HAVE BEEN FORCED OUT OF OUR ANCESTRAL HOME BY RELATIVES, AND THEIR CASE IS STILL PENDING IN COURT.
I MUST LEAVE THIS PLACE AND MEET PEOPLE IN PERSON.

I MUST TRAVEL FROM THE HIMALAYAS TO KANYAKUMARI AND FROM GUJARAT TO BENGAL.
WHEREVER HE WENT, PEOPLE RUSHED TO HEAR HIM SPEAK.
HE TRULY SPEAKS THE INDIAN PHILOSOPHY.

WHAT IS IT? PLEASE FEEL FREE TO ASK ME ANYTHING.
SWAMI-JI, I'VE SEEN YOU PREACHING NONSTOP. I AM CONCERNED YOU MIGHT BE HUNGRY.
HAVE YOU BROUGHT SOMETHING FOR ME?
SWAMI-JI, HOW DO I ... I WILL UNDERSTAND IF YOU DON'T WANT TO ACCEPT FOOD FROM ME. I AM NOT FROM THE UPPER CASTE.

RELIGION AND CASTE SHOULD NOT MATTER TO ANYONE. WE ARE ALL ONE. I ACCEPT THE FOOD YOU'VE BROUGHT FOR ME—YOUR KINDNESS TRULY INSPIRES ME.

AT ANOTHER SUCH MEETING ...
SWAMI-JI, WHY DON'T YOU REPRESENT INDIA AT THE PARLIAMENT OF RELIGIONS IN CHICAGO?
IF IT IS THE DIVINE WILL, I WILL GO.

AT ALWAR, SWAMI-JI MEETS KING MANGAL SINGH.
WHY DO HINDUS WORSHIP STONES AND IDOLS? ISN'T IT FOOLISH?
IT IS NOT THE STONE WE WORSHIP, BUT WHAT IT REPRESENTS. IT IS A MEANS TO CONNECT WITH THE DIVINE.
SYMBOLS? IT'S NOTHING BUT SUPERSTITION!

THAT'S A PAINTING OF YOUR FATHER, ISN'T IT?
YES IT IS.
GO AHEAD, SPIT ON IT.
HOW DARE YOU SUGGEST SUCH A THING! THAT'S MY FATHER, I COULD NEVER INSULT HIM LIKE THAT.

IT'S JUST A PAINTING, NOT YOUR FATHER HIMSELF. YET IT REMINDS YOU OF HIM.
SIMILARLY, AN IDOL REMINDS US OF THE ALMIGHTY. IT IS A SYMBOL, NOT THE THING ITSELF.
SWAMI-JI, YOU HAVE OPENED MY EYES. I BOW TO YOU..

I HAVE TRAVELLED THE LENGTH AND BREADTH OF INDIA. FOR MANY, EVEN SECURING TWO MEALS A DAY IS A STRUGGLE. SOMEONE MUST CARRY THE MESSAGE OF INDIA AND SPREAD IT ACROSS THE WORLD.

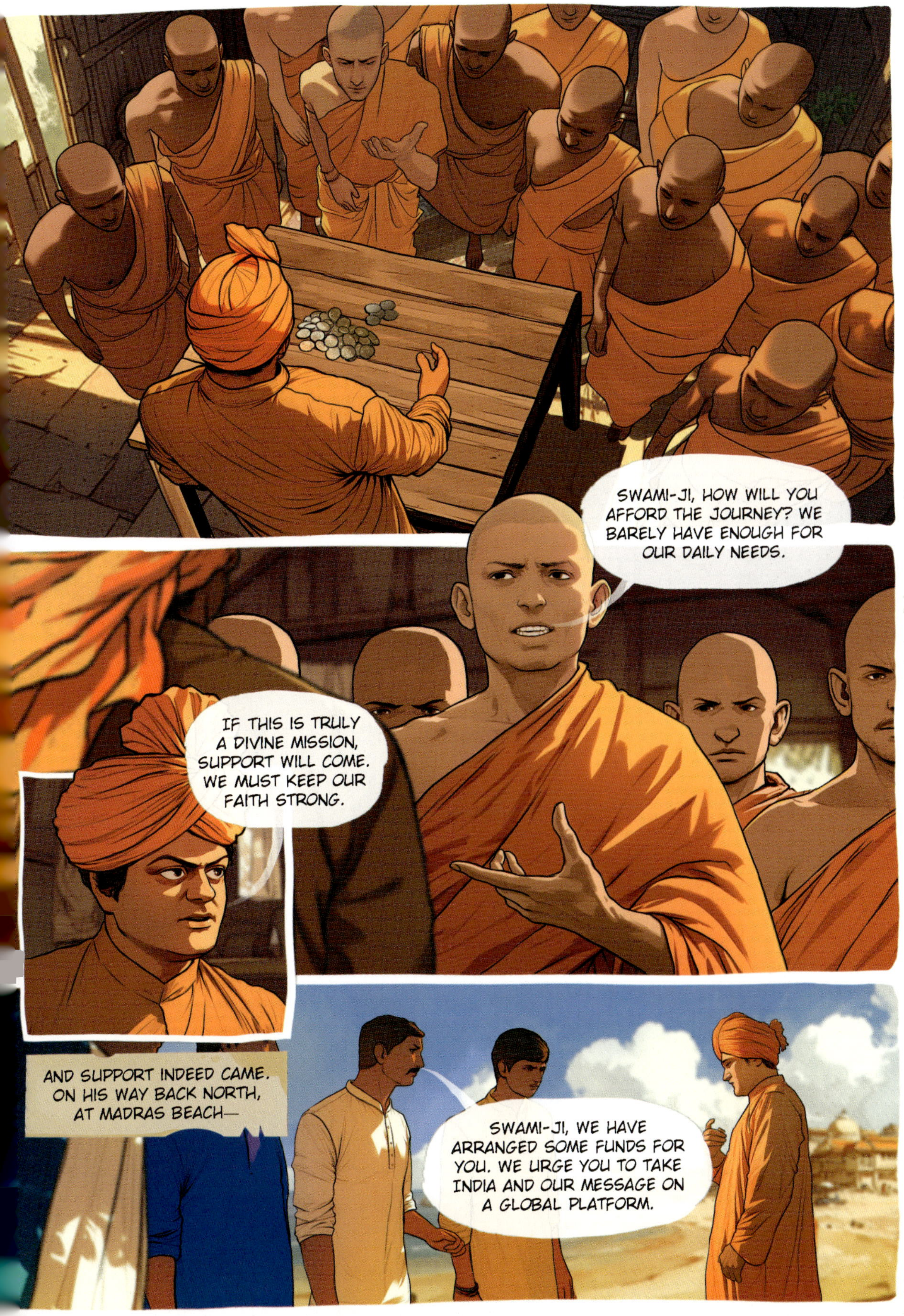
SWAMI-JI, HOW WILL YOU AFFORD THE JOURNEY? WE BARELY HAVE ENOUGH FOR OUR DAILY NEEDS.
IF THIS IS TRULY A DIVINE MISSION, SUPPORT WILL COME. WE MUST KEEP OUR FAITH STRONG.
AND SUPPORT INDEED CAME. ON HIS WAY BACK NORTH, AT MADRAS BEACH—
SWAMI-JI, WE HAVE ARRANGED SOME FUNDS FOR YOU. WE URGE YOU TO TAKE INDIA AND OUR MESSAGE ON A GLOBAL PLATFORM.

SWAMI-JI, WHAT IF THEY DON'T UNDERSTAND OUR TEACHINGS? IT COULD BE HUMILIATING.
OUR MESSAGE IS ETERNAL. IT IS NOT MINE, BUT INDIA'S. IF EVEN ONE SOUL AWAKENS, IT WILL HAVE BEEN WORTH THE EFFORT.
NARENDRANATH MEETS MAHARAJA AJIT SINGH BAHADUR OF KHETRI IN PANCHPANA, RAJASTHAN.
SWAMI-JI, PLEASE ACCEPT MY HUMBLE DONATION FOR YOUR TRIP. YOUR WORDS WILL INSPIRE MILLIONS.
THAT'S VERY GENEROUS OF YOU, MAHARAJ.

I REQUEST THAT YOU TAKE THE NAME VIVEKANANDA, A UNION OF TWO WORDS—VIVEK AND ANAND, SYMBOLISING THE BLISS OF WISDOM.
AND SO, THE KING OF KHETRI BESTOWED A NEW NAME UPON THE MONK—VIVEKANANDA.
THUS, SWAMI VIVEKANANDA JOURNEYED ACROSS THE SEAS TO CHICAGO TO PARTICIPATE IN THE PARLIAMENT OF THE WORLD'S RELIGIONS.
VOYAGES ARE MORE THAN JOURNEYS ACROSS SEAS.
THEY ARE GATEWAYS TO NEW EXPERIENCES.

SOMETIMES, A SINGLE VOYAGE CAN TRANSFORM NOT JUST ONE LIFE, BUT THE COURSE OF MANY.
I MUST TAKE THIS TRAIN FROM VANCOUVER TO REACH THE CITY OF CHICAGO.

THERE'S SOMETHING REMARKABLE ABOUT THIS MONK. HE RADIATES A SPIRITUAL AURA—I MUST SPEAK WITH HIM.
GLAD TO MEET YOU SIR. MAY I ASK, WHERE ARE YOU TRAVELLING TO?
I AM VISITING CHICAGO FOR THE PARLIAMENT OF THE WORLD'S RELIGIONS.
LIFE'S GREATEST LESSONS OFTEN DON'T COME FROM THE DESTINATIONS WE PLAN.
HERE IS MY CARD. IF YOU GET TIME, I WOULD BE HONOURED TO HAVE YOU AS A GUEST AT MY HOME IN METCALF, MASSACHUSETTS.
SURE. THANK YOU FOR THE INVITATION.

... BUT FROM THE CHALLENGES WE FACE ALONG THE WAY.
REGISTRATION
WHAT? ARE YOU SURE?
YES, SIR. THE PARLIAMENT OF THE WORLD'S RELIGIONS HAS BEEN POSTPONED TO SEPTEMBER.
MOREOVER, YOU MUST BE SPONSORED BY A RECOGNISED ORGANISATION TO ATTEND. NO ONE WITHOUT CREDENTIALS FROM AN ACCREDITED ORGANISATION WILL BE ACCEPTED AS A DELEGATE! AND THE LETTER YOU PRESENTED IS NOT FROM AN ACCREDITED ORGANISATION.
POSTPONED? I NEED A BONAFIDE SPONSOR ... WHERE WILL I FIND ONE IN THIS FOREIGN LAND?

WHAT WILL I DO HERE NOW?
KINDNESS CAN BE FOUND IN THE STRANGEST OF LANDS.

PLEASE STAY HERE WITHOUT ANY HESITATION. I'D LIKE TO INTRODUCE YOU TO FRANKLIN BENJAMIN SANBORN AND PROF. J.H. WRIGHT. PERHAPS THEY CAN HELP RESOLVE YOUR ISSUE WITH FINDING A BONA FIDE ORGANISATION.
AFTER HEARING SWAMI VIVEKANANDA'S COMPLETE STORY ...
I AM A PROFESSOR AT HARVARD. PLEASE DON'T WORRY, I SHALL WRITE TO THE SELECTION COMMITTEE OF THE PARLIAMENT.
YOUR KINDNESS IS BEYOND WORDS. THANK YOU.
YOU HAVE BEEN ACCEPTED AS A DELEGATE TO THE PARLIAMENT OF THE WORLD'S RELIGIONS.
SOON THE NEWS FINALLY ARRIVED. SWAMI VIVEKANANDA WAS NOW A RECOGNISED DELEGATE.

SWAMI VIVEKANANDA RETURNS TO CHICAGO, BUT ...
SIR, THE ROOM COSTS $2 PER NIGHT.
OH! THIS IS TOO EXPENSIVE. AT THIS RATE, I WILL EXHAUST MY FUNDS VERY SOON.
LOOK AT HIS CLOTHES! I'VE NEVER SEEN ANYTHING LIKE THIS BEFORE!
WHERE COULD HE BE FROM?
THEIR STARES DON'T BOTHER ME. MY MISSION IS GREATER THAN THIS DISCOMFORT.
BRRR ... THE NIGHTS ARE GETTING VERY COLD. I DON'T HAVE THE PROPER CLOTHES FOR THIS WEATHER.

DAYS GO BY ...
GURU-JI, WITH YOUR BLESSINGS, I HAVE MADE IT HERE. TODAY IS THE DAY I AM TO ADDRESS THE AUDIENCE.
THE VENUE IS GRAND, PACKED WITH SCHOLARS FROM ALL OVER THE WORLD.
SOME PEOPLE MAY BE SCEPTICAL OF ME TODAY, BUT THE HOPES OF MY ENTIRE COUNTRY REST ON MY SHOULDERS. I MUST DO MY BEST TO SPREAD GURUJI'S MESSAGE.
WHAT COULD THIS SWAMI POSSIBLY CONTRIBUTE TO THE DISCUSSION?
I HAVE MY DOUBTS TOO, BUT LET'S WAIT AND SEE.

IS HE AN INDIAN?
IS HE REALLY A MONK?
I WONDER WHAT THE MONK WILL SPEAK ABOUT.

SISTERS AND BROTHERS OF AMERICA ...
THERE ARE SCEPTICS, BUT AS SOON AS SWAMI VIVEKANANDA SPEAKS, THE AUDIENCE IS STUNNED INTO SILENCE.

IT FILLS MY HEART WITH JOY UNSPEAKABLE TO RISE IN RESPONSE TO THE WARM AND CORDIAL WELCOME WHICH YOU HAVE GIVEN US. I THANK YOU IN THE NAME OF THE MOST ANCIENT ORDER OF MONKS IN THE WORLD, I THANK YOU IN THE NAME OF THE MOTHER OF RELIGIONS, AND I THANK YOU IN THE NAME OF MILLIONS AND MILLIONS OF HINDU PEOPLE OF ALL CLASSES AND SECTS.

MY THANKS, ALSO, TO SOME OF THE SPEAKERS ON THIS PLATFORM WHO, REFERRING TO THE DELEGATES FROM THE ORIENT, HAVE TOLD YOU THAT THESE MEN FROM FAR-OFF NATIONS MAY WELL CLAIM THE HONOR OF BEARING TO DIFFERENT LANDS THE IDEA OF TOLERATION. I AM PROUD TO BELONG TO A RELIGION WHICH HAS TAUGHT THE WORLD BOTH TOLERANCE AND UNIVERSAL ACCEPTANCE.
WE BELIEVE NOT ONLY IN UNIVERSAL TOLERATION, BUT WE ACCEPT ALL RELIGIONS AS TRUE. I AM PROUD TO BELONG TO A NATION WHICH HAS SHELTERED THE PERSECUTED AND THE REFUGEES OF ALL RELIGIONS AND ALL NATIONS OF THE EARTH. I AM PROUD TO TELL YOU THAT WE HAVE GATHERED IN OUR BOSOM THE PUREST REMNANT OF THE ISRAELITES, WHO CAME TO SOUTHERN INDIA AND TOOK REFUGE WITH US IN THE VERY YEAR IN WHICH THEIR HOLY TEMPLE WAS SHATTERED TO PIECES BY ROMAN TYRANNY.
I AM PROUD TO BELONG TO THE RELIGION WHICH HAS SHELTERED AND IS STILL FOSTERING THE REMNANT OF THE GRAND ZOROASTRIAN NATION. I WILL QUOTE TO YOU, BRETHREN, A FEW LINES FROM A HYMN WHICH I REMEMBER TO HAVE REPEATED FROM MY EARLIEST BOYHOOD, WHICH IS EVERY DAY REPEATED BY MILLIONS OF HUMAN BEINGS:
"AS THE DIFFERENT STREAMS HAVING THEIR SOURCES IN DIFFERENT PATHS WHICH MEN TAKE THROUGH DIFFERENT TENDENCIES, VARIOUS THOUGH THEY APPEAR, CROOKED OR STRAIGHT, ALL LEAD TO THEE."

THE ONCE SCEPTICAL CROWD, NOW RISES IN THUNDEROUS APPLAUSE.
CHICAGO DAILY NEWS
SEPTEMBER 1893
"A VOICE FROM INDIA: SWAMI VIVEKANANDA STEALS THE SHOW AT THE PARLIAMENT OF RELIGIONS"
I HAVE RECEIVED INVITATIONS TO LECTURE IN VARIOUS PARTS OF THE COUNTRY. THE MESSAGE IS SPREADING LIKE WILDFIRE.

FROM GRAND HALLS OF THE WEALTHY TO HUMBLE GATHERINGS OF THE POOR, FROM DEVOUT BELIEVERS TO SCEPTICAL ATHEISTS, SWAMI VIVEKANANDA'S MESSAGE OF UNITY AND TOLERANCE ECHOES ACROSS THE DIVERSE LANDSCAPE OF AMERICA.

I HAVE GOTTEN A LETTER FROM CALCUTTA. THEY ARE HONOURING ME FOR MY CONTRIBUTIONS. IT IS TRULY HUMBLING.
I HAVE ALSO RECEIVED INVITATIONS FROM THE UNITED KINGDOM. I MUST ALSO VISIT THERE.
MY DAYS AND NIGHTS ARE NO LONGER MINE, BUT RATHER FOR THE MISSION OF SPREADING THE MESSAGE.
1895 NOVEMBER, LONDON
WHILE IN LONDON, SWAMI VIVEKANANDA IS INVITED TO EXPLAIN VEDANTA PHILOSOPHY IN THE DRAWING ROOM OF AN ARISTOCRATIC FAMILY.

AMONG THE GUESTS ARE MARGARET, AND HER COLLEAGUE FROM THE RUSKIN SCHOOL, EBENEZER COOKE.
VEDANTA IS NOT A DOGMA; IT IS THE SCIENCE OF THE SOUL, THE ULTIMATE TRUTH THAT TRANSCENDS TIME, CULTURE AND CREED. IT TEACHES US THAT DIVINITY RESIDES WITHIN EACH OF US—BEYOND ALL IDENTITIES, BEYOND ALL LABELS.
MARGARET HAS COME OUT OF CURIOSITY, UNAWARE THAT THIS ENCOUNTER WOULD CHANGE HER LIFE.
I HAVE EXPLORED EASTERN TEACHINGS BEFORE, BUT THE WAY SWAMIJI EXPLAINS THEM IS TRULY MESMERISING. THE WORDS OF SWAMI VIVEKANANDA HAVE COME TO US LIKE LIVING WATER, QUENCHING THE THIRST OF THOSE WHO WERE PERISHING.
TAT TVAM ASI ...

SWAMI VIVEKANANDA IS NOW ON HIS WAY BACK TO INDIA.
ENROUTE TO INDIA, SWAMI VIVEKANANDA HAS A STOP AT COLOMBO, WHERE HE IS IN FOR A SURPRISE.
VICTORY TO SWAMI VIVEKANANDA!
VICTORY TO SWAMI VIVEKANANDA!
I AM TRULY GRATEFUL FOR THIS HONOUR.
I AM NOW RESTLESS TO REACH MY MOTHERLAND.

HIS ARRIVAL IN INDIA IS A MONUMENTAL EVENT, CELEBRATED AS A NATIONAL TRIUMPH.
VICTORY TO SWAMI VIVEKANANDA!
SWAMIJI, WE SEEK YOUR BLESSINGS.

LATER ...
I WANT ALL OF US TO DEDICATE OUR LIVES TO SPREAD THE MESSAGE AND CARE FOR THE POOR AND SICK.
HIS DREAM IS COMING TRUE.
WE ARE THE LAND OF THE VEDAS, UPANISHADS, AND THE BHAGAVAD GITA! WE HAVE GIVEN THE WORLD LIGHT WHEN IT WAS LOST IN DARKNESS!
MY BROTHERS, IT IS NOT ENOUGH TO WORSHIP GOD IN TEMPLES OR THROUGH RITUALS. TRUE WORSHIP IS SERVING THOSE WHO NEED US—THE HUNGRY, THE SICK, THE POOR. THESE ARE THE LIVING IMAGES OF GOD.

ONE DAY, SWAMI VIVEKANANDA IS VISITED BY AN UNEXPECTED GUEST.
SWAMI-JI, I AM MARGARET. I HOPE YOU REMEMBER ME. I WANTED TO THANK YOU FOR WRITING TO ME AND ANSWERING MY QUESTIONS SO THOUGHTFULLY.
OF COURSE, MY SISTER. IT HAS BEEN MY DUTY.
I AM HERE TO LEARN MORE ABOUT INDIA—ITS HISTORY, ITS PEOPLE AND ITS SOUL. I WANT TO SERVE.
OUR HISTORY, OUR LITERATURE, OUR PHILOSOPHIES—THEY TELL THE STORY OF A CIVILISATION THAT HAS FLOURISHED FOR THOUSANDS OF YEARS. TO TRULY UNDERSTAND OUR CULTURE, YOU MUST KNOW THE LIVES OF BOTH THE COMMON PEOPLE AND THE GREAT PERSONALITIES WHO SHAPED THIS NATION—FROM ANCIENT SAGES TO MODERN REFORMERS.

SOON AFTER, TWO OF SWAMI VIVEKANANDA'S FEMALE DISCIPLES, SARA C. BULL AND JOSEPHINE MACLEOD, ARRIVE FROM AMERICA.
THANK YOU, SWAMI-JI, FOR ALLOWING US TO COME HERE TO SERVE.
THEY QUICKLY FORM A LIFELONG BOND WITH MARGARET.
11 MARCH 1898, STAR THEATRE, CALCUTTA
ENGLAND HAS SENT US ANOTHER GIFT IN THE FORM OF MISS MARGARET NOBLE.
I AM HUMBLED, SWAMI-JI. I AM HERE TO SERVE INDIA AND ITS PEOPLE.

LATER ...
ON 25 MARCH 1898, MARGARET IS GETTING FORMALLY INITIATED IN THE VOW OF BRAHMACHARYA, AT NILAMBAR MUKHERJEE GARDEN, HOWRAH.
FROM THIS DAY FORWARD, YOU SHALL BE CALLED NIVEDITA—THE DEDICATED ONE.
THANK YOU, SWAMI-JI.
GO FORTH AND FOLLOW HIM, WHO WAS BORN AND GAVE HIS LIFE FOR OTHERS COUNTLESS TIMES BEFORE HE ATTAINED THE VISION OF THE BUDDHA.
SWAMI VIVEKANANDA ENTRUSTED HER WITH THE MISSION OF EDUCATING INDIA'S WOMEN, A TASK SHE WOULD PURSUE WITH UNWAVERING DEDICATION.

SWAMI VIVEKANANDA CONTINUES HIS TRAVELS AND REACHES THE SACRED SITE OF AMARNATH.
IN THIS SACRED PLACE, WHERE TIME STANDS STILL, I FEEL THE PRESENCE OF THE ETERNAL. THIS IS WHERE THE GREAT LORD SHIVA RESIDES, THE DESTROYER OF IGNORANCE, THE SOURCE OF INFINITE KNOWLEDGE.

WE WILL ESTABLISH CENTRES ASSOCIATED WITH THE RAMAKRISHNA ORDER, SPREAD ACROSS THE WORLD—FROM THE INDIAN SUBCONTINENT TO EUROPE AND AFRICA TO AMERICA.
WITH HIS MISSION SPREADING ACROSS CONTINENTS, SWAMI VIVEKANANDA CONTINUES TO VISIT SPIRITUAL CENTRES IN THE WEST, WHERE HIS TEACHINGS TOUCH COUNTLESS LIVES.

WHILE SWAMI VIVEKANANDA CONTINUES HIS MISSION, HIS HEALTH SLOWLY STARTED TO DETERIORATE.
ON 4 JULY 1902, AFTER SHARING A SIMPLE MEAL WITH HIS DISCIPLES, SWAMI VIVEKANANDA FEELS AN UNUSUAL PEACE SETTLE OVER HIM ...
MY WORK HERE IS DONE. I MUST NOW RETURN TO MY TRUE SELF.
AT 7 O'CLOCK IN THE EVENING ...
I MUST QUIETLY RETIRE TO MY ROOM FOR MEDITATION.

HE SITS IN DEEP MEDITATION, ENTERING A STATE OF PROFOUND SILENCE.
THE BODY IS BUT A VEHICLE.
MY SOUL IS NOW FREE. O LORD, I RETURN TO THEE.

TIME STOOD STILL. THE SILENCE IS DEEP.
SWAMI-JI? ARE YOU ALRIGHT?
THE DISCIPLES FOUND THEIR BELOVED TEACHER IN PERFECT PEACE. SWAMI VIVEKANANDA ENTERED MAHASAMADHI, HIS SOUL MERGING WITH THE INFINITE.

VIVEKANANDA IS NOW RECOGNISED AS ONE OF THE MOST INFLUENTIAL PHILOSOPHERS AND SOCIAL REFORMERS IN CONTEMPORARY INDIA, AND ONE OF THE MOST SUCCESSFUL MISSIONARIES OF VEDANTA TO THE WESTERN WORLD. HIS LEGACY ENDURES, INSPIRING GENERATIONS ACROSS THE GLOBE.

LEARN EVERYTHING THAT IS GOOD FROM OTHERS, BUT BRING IT IN AND IN YOUR OWN WAY ABSORB IT. DO NOT BECOME OTHERS.
-SWAMI VIVEKANANDA.

OUR RECENT LAUNCHES

MUNSHI
PREMCHAND
DIVINE JUSTICE | A TALE OF TWO OXEN

STORIES FROM MY HEART
RUSKIN BOND

THE SIKH GURUS

THE STORY OF HANUMAN

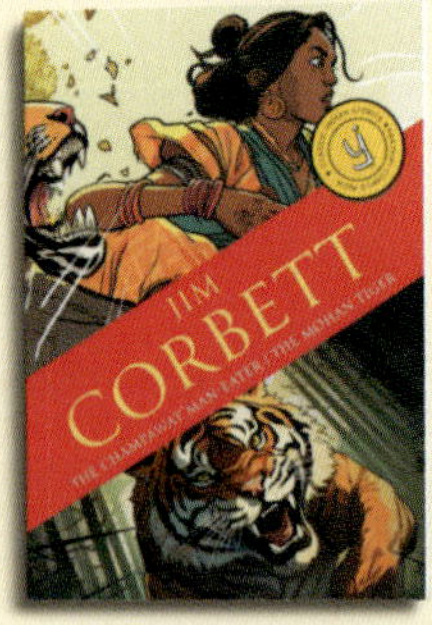

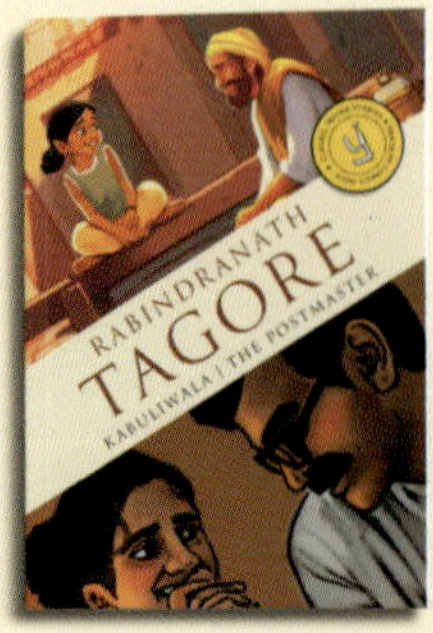

JIM
CORBETT
THE CHAMPAWAT MAN-EATER
THE MOHAN TIGER

SAADAT HASAN
MANTO
TOBA TEK SINGH |
THE DOG OF TITHWAL

RABINDRANATH
TAGORE
KABULIWALA | THE POSTMASTER

MUNSHI
PREMCHAND
EIDGAH | THE SALT INSPECTOR